SALAZAR SAYS...

Half a century or so after António de Oliveira Salazar's death, he has left behind a double legacy. On one hand, there is his notable work in government, based on fiscal balance, the independent and realistic handling of foreign policy, and his unwavering conviction regarding the place he believed Portugal should hold among nations.

On the other hand, there are the teachings, reflections, and essays characteristic of a statesman who was also a distinguished professor. In Salazar, two dimensions always coexisted: that of an experienced politician who, as a leader, had to make immediate decisions, and that of a theorist focused on analyzing social dynamics.

This book, happily reissued after so long, reveals the quality and fairness of the great Portuguese head of state as a thinker capable of reflecting not only on the historical period he was destined to live in but also, if I may say, sub specie aeternitatis (from the perspective of eternity).

—**VICENTE MASSOT**, Doctor in Political Science

At the dawn of the 21st century, the political and intellectual legacy of António de Oliveira Salazar has garnered renewed attention among those who critique the enduring progressive inclination toward dismantling traditional structures. Today, Salazar's influence is invoked not so much in relation to the authoritarian aspects of his regime but rather as a touchstone for certain principles and ideals.

Echoing a significant strand within historiography, leading intellectuals of Christian conservatism challenge reductive characterizations of Salazar as a mere symbol of so-called "eternal fascism." Instead, they regard his thought as a considered embodiment of European intellectual tradition, underscoring the enduring importance of religious spirituality as a counterbalance to materialist secularism in politics, the value of community identity rooted in historical continuity as opposed to fragmented individualism, and a resolute defense of Western civilization against the tides of deconstruction.

Today, Salazar's reflections continue to offer a valuable framework for those who, undeterred by anachronistic interpretations, seek to engage with and critique the dominant liberal paradigm in a substantive and reflective manner.

—**RICCARDO MARCHI**, Researcher, Center for International Studies — ISCTE-IUL (Lisbon)

SALAZAR

PRIME MINISTER OF PORTUGAL

SAYS...

Foreword by
MARCOS PINHO DE ESCOBAR

AROUCA
PRESS

Originally published by SPN Books (Lisbon) in 1939.

ISBN: 978-1-998492-28-2

Arouca Press
PO Box 55003
Bridgeport PO
Waterloo, ON
N2J 0A5
Canada
www.aroucapress.com
Send inquiries to info@aroucapress.com

CONTENTS

Introduction (1939) xi

Foreword xv

PRINCIPLES and ACTION 1

STATE and REGIMES 9

ORDER and GOVERNMENT 19

MEN and NATION 31

PRODUCTION and WORK 37

OUR NATIONALISM 51

THE PORTUGUESE EMPIRE 63

PORTUGAL in WORLD 69

Alphabetical Index 77

INTRODUCTION (1939)

THE following pages contain two hundred thoughts selected from the writings of Salazar.

The phrases here collected are quoted from speeches, preambles, official Notes and other fragmentary writings which prove the activity of the Leader of the Portuguese Recovery.

They are not an epitome of a treatise on the art of governing nations, which Salazar had never thought of writing. But they are the incidental expression of his thoughts on essential problems which have attracted the statesman's attention. But even apart from this fundamental distinction, one may say that the collection which we present is incomplete. It is incomplete by virtue of the very nature of the writings from which it has been derived.

The expression of Salazar's though is essentially logical. Thus in his speeches, problems are examined and summarized in a spirit of the most penetrating analysis and the solutions are deduced with an almost mathematical precision. From that very cause, the reasoning is so close that it is often impossible to isolate any one phrase to sum up a practical suggestion or constructive theory.

In their entirety, the speeches of Salazar form a political philosophy in which are discussed nearly all the vital problems that today, in internal and external affairs, occupy the thoughts of the leaders of a nation.

It is precisely because their author detests dogmatic statements, which owe whatever value they may possess to the emphatic tone in which they are made, that the writings of Salazar frequently do not lend themselves to a selection of suggestive maxims. They are based on logic, and logic cannot be broken up.

For that very reason a knowledge of the entire texts would be required in order to set forth on innumerable questions the thought of the Portuguese National Revolution, which Salazar embodies. It would be necessary to study the whole of the speeches, notes and preambles which bear witness to his extraordinary activity.

Nevertheless we consider that a publication of this kind is not useless, since it will enable the reader in a few pages to appreciate the points of view of the man who inspired the movement of renewal which marks a new era in Portugal.

Moreover Salazar's thought is so uniformly consistent that, despite the necessarily incomplete character of this collection, in so far as one may deduce the particular from the general and apply a theory to a concrete instance, it constitutes the summary of a political, economic and social doctrine, the doctrine which made the regeneration of Portugal possible.

The very fact of its uncompromising nationalism prevents it from supplying a doctrine to be exported as a remedy for the universal ills that afflict mankind. But it is nonetheless of great interest to understand the particular case of Portugal in the light of the spirit which presided over the solution of its difficulties. To know Salazar's thought is to possess the indispensable basis for the understanding of a whole page of the history of Portugal.

FOREWORD

THE following pages, which can almost be considered a collection of aphorisms, contain two hundred thoughts extracted from the writings of a scholar-turned-statesman. They reflect ideas, concepts and principles that are essential to the Art and Science of good government. They are the words of a wise man. They are the words of António de Oliveira Salazar.

Seminarian, Law student at the old University of Coimbra, professor of Political Economy and Finance at the same institution, Catholic intellectual, Portugal's Finance Minister (1928–1932) and Prime Minister (1932–1968), Salazar exerted a profound and extended impact on national life.

Appointed Finance Minister in a desperate attempt to save Portugal from financial bankruptcy, the young and eminent professor accomplished his mission in a spectacular fashion. In just one year public accounts were restructured and in surplus, remaining healthy and stable for decades to come, allowing foreign and domestic debt to be paid off or sharply reduced, interest rates to fall, gold reserves to increase dramatically and the Escudo to appreciate and stabilise, becoming one of the world's strongest currencies. A healthy financial position opened the path to economic reforms that would lead to real and sustainable social development.

Four years after Salazar assumed as Finance Minister, in a context of financial, economic and social stability, the military that had put an end to the mayhem of a Jacobin republic saw the urge to institutionalise a new political regime. Unanimous in what they rejected, namely the permanent state of civil war produced by the party system and parliamentarian factions, the armed forces and their supporting civilian sectors could not agree on and conceive a comprehensive and consistent political alternative.

The obvious choice for the daunting task was Salazar. As the most prestigious person in government, having established his natural authority as a result of his impressive accomplishments, technical knowledge, as well as his personal and work ethic, he had long reflected on the State and its problems and had a precise vision for a new political architecture.

Exercising power that was delegated to him by the military, and supported by a broad-based civilian front, the former Coimbra academic was constrained to mediate a balanced solution in order to guarantee the fundamentals he deemed absolutely necessary for the new political order. God and virtue, the Fatherland and its history, authority and its prestige, the family and its moral, the glory of work and the duty to work, were Salazar's non-negotiable pillars of the Estado Novo.

Contemporary of other attempts to tackle the weaknesses and failures of the modern State, and derived from the counterrevolutionary critique, the new political construction aimed to transcend liberal democracy and socialism while simultaneously rejecting the totalitarian option. It materialised in the establishment of a Catholic-oriented, corporatist and nationalist State, in which authority is decidedly strong but is limited by morality and law.

This "fourth position" — generally classified by political scientists as National Catholicism — assured over four decades of order, peace, stability and real progress for the Portuguese people. It provided a framework through which the country could be painstakingly restored, both spiritually and materially, in an endeavour that was "wholeheartedly" blessed and praised by Pope Pius XII as a "glorious enterprise."

Salazar is convinced that Catholic doctrine provides the conditions for order in the political society, an order that is absolutely essential to its very existence, prosperity and conservation. Therefore the State, established to secure the common good, must be ordered to a transcendental end — it must be ordered to God.

The concept of the common good is paramount in the statesman's political thought and everything else will derive from this notion. He sees it as the sole aim of the exercise of power, as the raison d´être of government, as the sacred function of politics, written with a capital "P". And how does Salazar perceive the common good in practical terms? It is what could be called the complete common good: the legitimate material well-being ordered to a virtuous life and both, in turn, ordered to the salvation of the souls. In other words: he believes it is the duty of the State to secure adequate moral and material conditions, so that men are able to earn a decent and honourable living on this earth, and on this earth obtain eternal life in heaven.

Salazar's political concepts were never subjected to systematization or published as a treatise, but were gradually spelled out in speeches pronounced pari passu with government action. "Pieces of prose that were said," "imposed by circumstances," as he wrote in the preface of the first volume of his works, these speeches presented political concepts as he dealt with concrete matters.

Published between 1934 and 1967, the six volumes of *Discursos e Notas Políticas* contain the writings of Salazar as Finance Minister and Prime Minister, presenting his complete thought on political, economic and social issues. In 1997, twenty-seven years after his passing, the printing of *Inéditos e Dispersos*, a five-volume collection of texts, conferences and articles produced as a seminarian, student, professor and Catholic intellectual, provide valuable insights into the origins and development of his political philosophy.

In this body of work six main theoretical sources can be identified: the Encyclicals of Popes Leo XIII and Saint Pius X, with their distinctive social-political themes; the social-catholic doctrine of Frédéric Le Play; the political Catholicism of René de la Tour-du-Pin; the works of social psychologist Gustave Le Bon; and — very especially — the "integral nationalism" theorised by Charles Maurras, head of Action française.

These solid foundations, naturally complemented by other authors who left a mark on Salazar, were processed and further developed by his personal reflection on the crisis of the modern State, with meticulous consideration of historical circumstances and concrete political experience.

The starting point of Salazar's political thinking is the fundamental phenomenon of order. In this particular case, it starts out as a reaction to and a rejection of the appalling instability — the "general disorder" — of the Portuguese Republic and the blatant incapacity of the State to fulfil its first duty, which is to be the guarantor of order.

It is important to notice that Salazar's reflections are not meant to be a universal blueprint. His refusal of standardised formulas or doctrines with global applicability was well known. The objective was to elaborate a synthesis tailored to the specific character of the Portuguese nation, considered in her historical origin and destiny.

Applying the very Maurrasian method of "organizing empiricism," Salazar carefully scrutinises History and concrete political experiences so as to determine and confirm what is true and permanent in the governing of peoples. On the one hand he sets apart what is naturally characteristic of men, ingrained in their souls, from what is deemed erroneous, superficial or accessory, and which are only present in some circumstances. On the other hand he separates cause and effect of political action, while objectively comparing the practical results of doctrines with government procedures. In other words, given the particular conditions of Portuguese life, what Salazar is looking for in historical experience is to determine what factors are responsible for the maintenance of order in political society – an order, the objective of which can only be the common good.

This book, albeit a glimpse into a substantial work, is a good introduction to Salazar's thought on essential political, economic and social matters. It contains excerpts that, far from being merely abstract notions, reflect the underlying principles of actual policies and government actions that passed the empirical test and the test of time. Relevant in 1939, the ideas presented in these pages are perhaps even more pertinent today.

In a time when ideology, narratives and self-perceptions of all sorts seem to have taken the place of reality, there is much to be gained from a political thinker whose reflections are firmly rooted in reality. By doing so Salazar was able to preserve and exercise a rational faculty that has been practically extinguished by the perverse action of ideologies: common sense, or the natural ability to see things as they really are and do things as they should really be done. And with common sense came political prudence. In a world where political activity is mostly reduced to a brutal competition for power by corrupt and demagogic factions, Salazar reminds us that Politics is a moral reality and that it exists to serve men — therefore, its fundamental laws must derive from the depths of human nature. In an age of radical materialism, individualism and hedonism, this Portuguese thinker recalls the primacy of spirit over matter and that men have an immortal soul and a supernatural destiny. And if God has been "cancelled" from political life, lets reassert with Salazar that the State should be "God's Ministry for the common good".

Marcos Pinho de Escobar
Monte Estoril, October 2024

*Men of good faith know that I always
speak to them with perfect sincerity.*

PRINCIPLES
and
ACTION

FAITH

ONE must examine in doubt, then act with faith.

ONE cannot govern in the name of doubt.

CONFIDENCE

THE country feels in its innermost heart the value of the work undertaken; a breath of heroism has thrilled it; for we have made it sufficiently clear that there is no longer any place among us for the timid or the skeptical.

CERTAINTIES

TO spirits torn by the doubt and negativism of the age, we seek to restore the solace of the great certainties. We do not discuss God or virtue; we do not discuss our country or its history; we do not discuss authority and its prestige; we do not discuss the family and its ethics; we do not discuss the glory and duty of labour.

DIFFICULTIES

THE man who possesses pride and self-respect only feels real joy when he overcomes great difficulties. Little difficulties do not affect a man's life and cannot give him the consciousness and true joy of having fulfilled his duty.

I HAVE always been in favour of a policy of plain good sense, as opposed to a policy of magnificent plans, plans so vast and magnificent that all our energy was spent in admiring them and there was no strength left to carry them out.

TRUTH, like authority, partakes of the nature of the absolute.

NO lying political school and system of government, but truth, truth in word and deed, in reforms and laws and in carrying them out.

I HAVE always been in favour of a policy of truth and of informing the people clearly of the situation of the country, in order to accustom them to the idea of sacrifices which must one day be made and which will be the heavier the longer they are delayed.

IN public as in private life, lack of sincerity displeases and wearies: no political regime which uses falsehood as a method of governing or contents itself with conventional truths can win the soul of the people.

IN throwing wide open, for examination and study by all competent persons, the doors of our house, of our institutions and services, we shall be equally grateful for praise and for criticism, since it is not our purpose to teach but rather to learn.

ONE must be true, and one must be just; I will even say that it is impossible to be loyal to truth without serving justice.

EVERY combatant must always have present in his mind, so as not to go astray or fail, that he only conquers who conquers with honour, that is to say, with truth and justice.

THAT man is strong who has reason on his side and gives others no ground to have reason against him.

THE thesis of responsibility admits of endless theoretic and abstract discussion; but the men on whose shoulders rests the burden of governing a nation learn from history or from their own experience that decadence coincides with certain morbid manifestations of the intellect and the will, with a claim to be free from the laws imposed on man and derived from his nature and purpose in life.

CORRUPTION easily creeps in when the responsibility of the few is replaced by the irresponsibility of the many.

IT is impossible that equal social worth should belong to him who builds and him who destroys, to one who educates and one who demoralizes, to the creators of civic or moral energies and the dreamers who hanker after degradation and decadence.

WE wish to inculcate a sense of duty and self-sacrifice, of justice and charity, in the methods of government, as a clear affirmation that morality must inspire all human actions, and inspire them the more intensely the greater is their influence or ascendancy over social life and the more numerous the ties that bind their author to other men.

THERE are tasks which require absolute devotion, the giving of one's whole self. For some natures such a task admits of no distraction.

SELF-SACRIFICE

ONE must receive the blows of life, calmly, endure the bitterness of adversity, follow one's destiny with faith, sacrifice oneself for the common good and disinterestedly, loyally, nobly, for one's country, feel the pride and the "glory of suffering".

IT is our duty to sacrifice everything for the sake of all; we are not called upon to sacrifice all of ourselves for the sake of a few.

SERIOUSNESS

THE seriousness of life does not necessarily imply gloom, pessimism or depression; it is not incompatible with the youthful gaiety of the people, with rejoicings, wit and laughter. It merely demands that serious things should be taken seriously.

GAIETY

GAIETY, cheerfulness, the joy of living, are energies which increase both the quality and the quantity of work produced.

IDEAS

IDEAS are not always capable of being realized or put into practical use; sometimes an idea is dead so far as action is concerned, and we cannot allow men to be chained to a corpse.

CHOICE

NOW, as in all critical times, it is necessary to choose, to know how to choose and to sacrifice the accidental to the essential, matter to spirit, grandeur to balance, wealth to justice, extravagance to economy, class strife to cooperation.

ACTION

NEGATION, indifference and doubt can never be the springs of action, and life is action.

WILL

THERE are no insoluble problems for a nation which knows how to will.

TENACITY

I HAVE accustomed the Portuguese people to face calmly and resolutely the problems which affect its collective life, and I do not repent of having done so. If there are obstacles, difficulties, dangers, all the better: in meeting and overcoming them the temper of an individual and of a people is tempered and strengthened; not may we flinch before tasks which, after all, are not so great as those which were accomplished by our ancestors. And we are still the same nation, the same race, the same people.

STATE
and
REGIMES

THE state should always be a man of honour.

THE state has regard to doctrine, not to persons; therefore its authority or consent cannot be invoked to cover up errors, abuses, injustices, deficiencies, which are contrary to its true spirit.

IF the state is a theory in action, it is not logical that it should abandon its own doctrine, but rather it must spread and defend it, since in doing so it is working to consolidate itself.

THE state has the right to foster, harmonize and control all national activities, without destroying them and its duty to educate the youth in the love of their country, in discipline and those vigorous exercises which will prepare and incline it for a fruitful activity and for all that may be required of it by the honour and interests of the nation.

THE state, whatever may be its form, is in itself the political structure derived from a system of fundamental concepts, of a certain number of answers to questions which lie at the base of the whole of social life: the idea and value of the nation, the idea of human personality and its rights, of the purpose of human life and of the extent and limitations of authority.

POWER OF THE STATE

NO one in Portugal would maintain the omnipotence of the State with regard to the mass of mankind, which is merely the raw material of great political achievements. No one here would think of regarding the State as the source of morality and justice without submitting its rules and decisions to the decrees of a higher justice. No one here would dare to proclaim might as the source of all right, without regard for individual conscience and the legitimate liberties of the citizen and the purpose inherent in the very existence of a man.

STATE AND MORALITY

THE state must be strong, but it must be limited by the demands of morality, by the principles of men's rights, by individual guarantees and liberties, which are the first and foremost condition of social solidarity.

STATE AND GOVERNMENT

THERE can be no strong state without a strong government.

THE SOVEREIGNTY OF THE NATION

TO take power out of the hands of party cliques; to place above all individual interests the interests of all, the interests of the nation; to keep the state from the clutches of audacious minorities but to maintain it in permanent touch with the needs and aspirations of the nation; to organize the nation from top to bottom in all the different manifestations of its collective life, from the family to the administrative bodies and moral and economic corporations; to incorporate all this in the state, which will thus become its living expression: this is to make the sovereignty of the nation a real and living thing.

REGIMES

ALL new regimes, lacking experience and even traditions, must be of slow and laborious growth. To apply new and different principles to old societies accustomed to living under another system, and especially with another spirit, is always a difficult task which even appears impossible to those who are in a hurry, and who feverishly demand that tomorrow's work should be done today.

LIBERALISM

LIBERALISM fell into this sophism: "There can be no liberty opposed to liberty." But in harmony with man's essential nature and with the realities of life we will rather say. "There can be no liberty opposed to the general interest."

STATE socialism is the bourgeois regime *par excellence*.

OUR recent experiment in democracy afforded no sure guarantee for the safety of individuals or of public liberties: the liberty of association, of public meetings, of the press, were in practice always subordinated to the interests of a government clique, with the aggravating circumstance that between the laws and the facts a great gulf was fixed and that the right to judge the legality or harmfulness of an action was not vested in any tribunal or regular court of justice but in the mob, as being the supporter of the government.

THE beauties of equality and the advantages of democracy have been so noised abroad and in exalting them the descent has been so rapid that a lower and lower level was reached, contrary to the fact of natural inequalities and the legitimate and necessary hierarchy of values in a well ordered society.

IN order to be wholeheartedly on the side of the people and to foster its steady material and moral improvement, we need not believe that the origin of power resides in the mass of the people, or that the justice of the laws is derived from mere numbers or that the government can be undertaken by the multitude and not by an elite whose duty it is to direct it and to sacrifice itself for the common good.

THREE FALLACIES

MANY said: Let us abandon the common weal to political passion, to the whims of the greatest number — life subordinated to politics — that was the democratic formula. There were others who cried: Let us produce wealth without care or method so that everyone in the end shall benefit — economic values were held higher than those of life under the liberal regime. Another group demanded: let us divide among ourselves the present wealth and that which may be created in our time — socialism subordinated economic life to social. The fallacy of these systems was amply demonstrated by the constant party warfare, the injustice of liberal economic life, the devastation worked by socialism.

STABILITY

THERE is no greater blessing for a nation, I think, than the stability of a good government; a stable government of nonentities means stagnation, but there is something worse: a rapid succession of geniuses, with their fragmentary ideas and plans and their reckless interference with the machinery of government.

THE REPRESENTATIVE SYSTEM

THE families, the parishes, the townships, the corporations, which include all citizens, with their fundamental legal rights, are the bodies which compose the nation, and, as such, must participate directly in the constitutions of the supreme organs of the state: this, more than any other, is the true expression of the representative system.

PARLIAMENTS

I FORESEE that parliaments in the future, even if they do not become purely political bodies, without any legislative character, will be obliged to approve only the general outlines of the more important laws, leaving to the executive, as responsible for the work of administration, far wider powers than the controlling power which it at present possesses.

CORPORATIVE CHAMBERS

THE formula which seems best and which will perhaps be the formula of the future, is that the government should legislate, in consultative collaboration with the corporative chambers, possibly with the assistance of a council of legal experts.

CRITICISM

THE government, a strong government, cannot prevent the publication of criticism of its acts. The government must defend itself not only against its enemies but against itself.

PUBLIC OPINION

GOVERNMENTS should never become the slaves of the public opinion of the masses, which is always inferior to and very different from the public opinion of the nation.

PUBLIC opinion is essential to the government of a people and sometimes a great stimulus, but in its own interests control over its formation must never be withdrawn.

PUBLIC opinion is indispensable to the life of any government. Governments, however strongly they may be supported, do not maintain themselves by employing force but by possessing it.

NEWSPAPERS

NEWSPAPERS are the spiritual food of the people, and, like all foods, must be controlled.

ORDER
and
GOVERNMENT

ORDER has always been the true condition of beauty.

AUTHORITY is a fact and a necessity: it only disappears in order to reappear; it is only attacked in order to give it into the hands of others. It is a right and a duty, a duty which betrays itself if it is not exercised, a right which has its best foundation in the common good. And it is also a high gift of Providence, since without it social life and human civilization would be alike impossible.

IN the family, the school, the church, the workshop, the syndicate, the barracks, the state, authority never exists for itself but for others; it is not a privilege but a burden.

THERE can be absolute authority; there can never be absolute liberty.

TRUE liberty can only exist in the spirit of man.

THE only possible kind of liberty is that which is guaranteed by the state and regulated by authority; a liberty which can lead,

I will not say to the happiness of man, but to the happiness of individual men.

THERE can be no liberty opposed to truth; there can be no liberty opposed to the general interest.

WIDE as may be our toleration towards differences of doctrine which divide men on many subjects, we are compelled to state that we do not admit liberty against the nation, against the common interest, against the family or against morality.

STRENGTH marches in fixed order and measured step: thus showing its inherent need of order in space and time; strength marches with head erect, revealing its confidence; strength advances with regular firm steps, it dominates and possesses the land through which it goes. Strength is true to itself, it "dies but does not surrender"; strength is unwearying, even in death, it "dies, but slowly".

INTRINSICALLY strength is brave, fearless, bold, dominating, self-possessed, conscious of its capacities and of its action; it is not disorderly, it is not exorbitant, it is not violent, It has time to impose itself: it is patient; it does not doubt itself: it is serene; it has the certainty of triumph: it is generous.

STRENGTH which is strength and not violence is essentially loyal, that is to say, true, straight forward and sincere. Note that strength marches to the sound of trumpets: it announces its presence; its arms shine in the sun: it displays its methods of attack; it commands in a loud voice: its intentions are made known.

OUR DOCTRINE

UNLIKE other movements in Europe which have preceded or succeeded ours, our doctrine is that of revolution.

REVOLUTIONS

ALL revolutions, small or great, embitter the life of a nation; it is always better to reform than to revolutionize, or to revolutionize through reform.

REVOLUTION

THE revolution must be not only profound in its aims but serious in its methods.

THE Revolution remains true to its original inspiration, unequivocally national, unreservedly spiritual, popular without servility or privilege. The nation continues to be the central point of all the acts of the government.

THE revolution has been an achievement inspired by what is high and great; and it suffices to be a Portuguese to realize the heroic significance of our regeneration.

WE have both a doctrine and a strength. With this strength we must govern; we have the mandate of a triumphant revolution, without opposition, and consecrated by our country; as followers of a doctrine, we must be uncompromising in its defence and in carrying out the principles which constitute it.

LAWS

LAWS may be judged by the principles which constitute them and by the general results of their application.

THE laws are in reality made by the men who carry them into effect, and beneath the veil of their purely abstract character, come to be in practice the mirror of our defects of understanding and errors of will.

GOVERNMENT

A GOVERNMENT may be defined as the continuous action of truth and justice.

THE motto of the Government is not to promise but to perform, not merely to begin but to fulfill.

FACED by the aspiring soul of the people, Governments, in their own defence, have to seek to excel themselves continually.

IN this task of reintegration and re-education, a task in which there is much to save that was being lost and much to build up and innovate, it is necessary at every step to compare principles and their application, institutions and their results, sacrifices and advantages, individual and collective reactions to reforms which run counter to customs and egoisms; we must remember what existed and what has ceased to exist, what was our aim and what has been our attainment, in order to be in a position to maintain or modify our attitude, to proceed or loyally to abandon a path of error. To this end and for the good of the people, politicians must have a good memory.

POLITICIANS must give heed to nothing that can hinder patriotic collaboration, to nothing that may lead them to repay injury with injury, to nothing that will impair their will to work or defile the clear well-spring of their good intentions.

OWING to the unbalanced spirit of man, order does not come spontaneously; it is necessary that someone should rule for the good of all, and that the choice should fall upon the man most capable of ruling.

EARNESTNESS, adaptation to circumstance, balance, independence, firmness tempered by flexibility, a knowledge of men and of their passions, the gift of gauging public opinion and of foreseeing the development of political and social events, disinterested devotion, complete surrender and sacrifice of self to the common good, by means of which must be redeemed all that there may have been of carelessness in the past, of neglect and folly, of irresponsible levity in the grim task of government; these are indispensable qualities for one who holds the highest post in the government of a nation.

POLITICS are necessary in the government of a nation, but to engage in politics is not to govern.

PERHAPS the policy of the government may now be better understood by many: when we insist that a sound finance is a necessary condition of the independence and integrity of our country; when we seek to bind together all true Portuguese in a really national unity; when we strive to awaken the country to a full consciousness of its worth and mission, so that it may be morally and materially prepared to be faithful to them when the time comes, these are no political phantasies but the best possible defence of the high interests of Portugal.

ADMINISTRATION

TRUE administration is always based in a conception of the state, of a social aim, of public authority and its limitations, of justice, of wealth and the functions of wealth in human societies; that is to say, in a political and economic doctrine, and, if you will, a philosophy.

ADMINISTRATIVE POLICY

I HAVE always been in favour of an administrative policy so clear and simple that it could be the work of any good housewife: a policy so ordinary and humble that it merely consists in spending well what one has to spend and in not living beyond one's income.

THE reform of the national finances is not only for us a factor of our political independence and a means of solving or attenuating the chief difficulties springing from the crisis; it is also the only sure foundation of economic reconstructions and of the organization of national defence.

SOUND finance is impossible without sound politics.

TO claim to cure the ills of the time by party pacts and the panaceas of political programs is to belittle the problem, for, if such methods could effectively vanquish the evil, there would be no reason why it should cause us so much anxiety.

NOT all political methods are suited to all times and all nations; statesmen have to proceed according to their nature and according to the realities of the day.

WORK which claims to be lasting must be careful throughout, it cannot be carried into effect impulsively.

BY the balance of our budget, the stabilization of our currency, our ordered economy, the social significance of our corporative organization, the progressive improvement of the conditions of labour, the education of the people, the reform of the state and the subordination of its activities to the supreme principles of morality and right; in strengthening the authority of the state without injuring the independence, dignity and liberties of the individual in the consistency and dignity of our public life, the calm affirmation of our independence and of our inalienable rights as a great colonial nation, we have not sought to give a lesson but merely an example.

MEN
and
NATION

WE live our life on earth and it is our duty to give it a meaning and a value.

LIFE is not a jest, but it need not be the heavy burden that some bear, bowed beneath a crushing weight, enslaved to a destiny which they cannot understand. It is, it should be considered merely as, a serious thing, and therefore it must have substance, it must be the most perfect realization possible of a certain ideal. In this sense each life ceases to be a mere passage of time and becomes an enduring achievement.

NATIONAL VALUES

THE worth of a nation lies not in the number of its inhabitants but rather in the qualities which they possess, their ability to create wealth, science, beauty, their capacity to toil and suffer, and the social discipline which enhances individual enterprise, renders great collective achievements possibly and induces a few to sacrifice themselves for the glory of all.

ESSENTIAL NEEDS

FROM the depths of human conscience spring clearly the following imperative needs: a life of work, ownership of the soil, virtue in the family, hope in the soul.

MEN are the essential element of the nation, which will be precisely what they are. Besides and perhaps above this, each man is a spirit and a conscience. How should we not respect and do our utmost to protect, elevate and improve that conscience and that spirit? A torturing problem: in this coexistence of man with society, of his mental and moral independence with the necessary authority of the state, how far must one go, how far can one go, so that individual man should not be diminished and the nation should grow strong and great in his own interest?

THE FAMILY

THE family is the purest source of the moral factors of production.

THE family can be extended to form the nation.

THE family, as the irreducible cell of society, the nucleus from which springs the parish, the township, and therefore the nation, is, by its very nature, the first of the organic political elements of the constitutional state.

WE do not discuss the family. In the family, man is born, the generations are brought up and that little world of affections is formed without which man could not easily exist. Destruction of the family entails destruction of the house, of the hearth, of the bonds of relationship, and men are left facing the state as isolated strangers, without roots, shorn of one half of their nature; they exchange a name for a number, and the life of society is essentially altered.

HOUSE AND FAMILY

THE intimacy of family life requires comfort and isolation, in a word it demands a house, an independent, private house or *our own*.

A SMALL independent house means quiet, tranquility, a legitimate sense of property, a family. A hive means promiscuity, revolution, hatred, the merging of the individual in the multitude.

EDUCATION

WE expect the family and the school to imprint indelibly on the souls of the young those high and noble sentiments which distinguish our civilization, and a deep love of their country and of those who made it and through the centuries raised it to greatness.

IT is essential that the spirit of the young should be guided by us in accordance with Portugal's historical vocation, by means of the examples in which our history abounds: examples of self-sacrifice, patriotism, abnegation, courage, a sense of personal dignity and unfailing respect for the dignity of others.

PHYSICAL EDUCATION

WE must defend the truth of life, which is toil and sacrifice and struggle and suffering, but which is also triumph, glory, joy, blue sky, open hearts and pure spirits; we must give the Portuguese, through the discipline of physical culture, the secret of keeping their youth, for the sake of Portugal.

THE SCHOOL

THE school is a sacred factory of souls.

WE could not conceive, we could not allow that the school, divorced from the nation, should not be at the service of the nation and should not realize the most important part assigned to it in this hour of regeneration, the task of research and instruction; of educating the Portuguese to understand and know how to work.

PRODUCTION *and* WORK

WE have maintained, and many foreign examples bear this out, that it is a pure illusion, to separate the social from the economic elements, as if the life of each one of us could be independent of labour and the production of wealth.

POLITICAL ECONOMY

THE whole structure of modern economy is profoundly shaken, and if there is delay in restoring its lost balance, speculation begins to take the place of business, finance dominates economy, and fantastic ideas destroy production, so that men and nations are uncertain whether they will gain or lose by producing and selling; and anarchy returns, and chaos and ruin.

WE wish to advance towards a new political economy, working in harmony with human nature, under the authority of a strong state which will protect the higher interests of the nation, its wealth and its labour, both from capitalist excesses and from destructive Bolshevism.

THE STATE AND ECONOMY

ONE cannot hope to constitute a strong and well-balanced state without coordinating and developing the national economy, which today more than ever must form part of political organization. This is perhaps the greatest practical constitutional change that must be effected in all civilized nations.

THE STATE AND PRODUCTION

THE state must maintain itself above the world of production, equally removed from absorbing it in monopolies and intervening in it through competition.

THE STATE AND WEALTH

THE state must not be the owner of the wealth of the nation nor allow itself to be corrupted by it. That it may be the supreme arbiter of all the interests of the nation it is imperative that it should not be a slave to any of them.

MONEY

MONEY is a delicate system, but it must be made to serve and not to command.

UP to the present time foreign money has been offered us and we have refused it; that is the whole truth of this matter.

CRISIS

IT is a moral rather than an economic crisis that is troubling the world.

THERE exists in the life of modern societies a crisis more serious than the crisis of currency, of exchanges of credit, or prices, of public finance; more serious because it is the source of all of them: the crisis in economic thought, that is, the crisis in the principles which underlie economic life.

THAT which is in crisis and which provokes the crisis is the exhaustion, neglect and disregard of the rules which govern human life, the breaking up of the moral structure of civilization; and the worst is that many think that they can invent other rules and impose them on the world.

ECONOMY IN THE SERVICE OF MAN

WEALTH, possessions, production are not ends in themselves; they have to serve both the individual and the collective interest; they are meaningless if they are not subordinated to the preservation and improvement of human life.

WE are not fascinated nor satisfied by wealth or mechanical luxury or inventions by which man is diminished, or by the mania for machinery, the colossal, immense, unique, mere brute force, unless they are touched by a breath of the spirit and subordinated to the service of rendering life ever more beautiful, more noble and more refined.

IMPROVEMENTS

MATERIAL and moral improvements, once they have been attained and have lost their novelty, do not generally weigh much on men's minds.

SOCIAL JUSTICE

SPIRIT naturally dominates matter by its intrinsic superiority and by a correct ordering of values, in education, work and the intimate meaning of life; the weaker, who are most exposed by their weakness to the ravages of fortune and to the abuses of the strong, have, in a well-considered justice, a special right to protection; and, unless their material situation be improved and their position in society and in the state transformed, our revolution will not have completed its task.

PLUTOCRATS

THE plutocrat is not the great industrial nor the financier; he is a hybrid species, a cross between political economy and finance; he is the "flower of evil" of the worst form of capitalism.

MODERN SLAVERY

IF man must not be a slave to riches, neither must he order his life in such a way that he is a slave to labour.

IT is not in the country (even in full crisis), where life is simple and without ambitions, that destitution becomes distressing and tragic. The hopeless tragedy is rather in the cities, in the great capitals, which become more insensitive and hard-hearted in proportion as they become more civilized. The mechanical and automatic character of progress which transforms men into machines keep them in brutal isolation, and substitute for the impulses of natural affection a cold and complicated mechanism. The man in cities, formed and shaped by the bitter struggle against others who contest his place in the sun, is, perhaps unconsciously, the very embodiment of egoism.

PROPERTY for the most part is a natural product, derived from the conditions of climate and geological formation, the possibilities of cultivation and the use made of them by the labour of man and the feats of machinery.

THE solidarity of interests which lies at the basis of society obliges each one of us to contribute with his intelligence or activity to the common good: the man who does not work injures all other men.

WORK, all work, possesses the same nobility and dignity, when it represents the contribution of each individual, according to his capacity, to the society to which he belongs.

SINCE it is the support of life, the origin of the wealth of nations and the source of the prosperity of people, work is a glory and an honour; it may differ in usefulness and economic value, but its moral dignity is always the same.

BY a gift of Providence work is necessary to our existence, and fortunately, with all our progress and accumulation of wealth, it will always be necessary to work in order to live; otherwise men would perish of weariness in a world of vice.

SINCE many men have no other means of living except their capacity to work, two consequences follow: one is that we must organize the economy of the nation in such a way that the workmen should have work; and the other is that work must be regulated and organized in such a way that the salaries of the workmen should allow them to live.

TO recognize labour as a factor in the cooperation of an enterprise and to associate it, therefore, morally and economically with the purpose of production, with due respect for the demands of property, profits and technical skill, is a doctrine which may likewise be consecrated by the state as fundamental, and on the realization of which progress in peace and order will largely depend.

THE WORKING CLASSES

WE wish to satisfy the claims of the working classes so far as order, justice and the balanced life of the nation allow; we will go farther, that is, than others proved capable of going who had promised to go all the way.

WE wish to protect the proletariat from their false prophets and to show that in our attitude there exists no economic question to divide us, but a different conception of life, a different idea of civilization.

WORKMEN'S FAMILIES

WE consider the regular existence of the workingman's family as both logical in social life and useful to the economy of the nation; we consider it essential that the workingman should support it; we hold that work for a married woman, and generally for an unmarried woman, with or without the responsibility of a family, should not be encouraged; there has never been a good housewife without plenty of work on her hands.

SALARIES

THE most suitable reward of labour consists of salaries. The workman may be associated in an enterprise, he may have an interest in its results, that is to say, in its profits; but those who have no means of subsistence cannot wait nor speculate nor live without being paid; that is why the ideal that must underlie every possible scheme must be a sufficient salary.

CLASS STRIFE

WE do not accept the strife of the productive classes as a historical fact nor as the principle underlying economic and social organization. The ultimate interests, both of individuals and groups, tend towards identity of national interests. But the immediate interests of workmen and employers, and sometimes of the workmen among themselves, often clash in actual life; all the more reason not to allow the discord to grow, all the more reason to reconcile opposing interests, to the advantage of both parties and with a view to normalize the economic life of the nation.

COMMUNISM is the synthesis of all the traditional revolts of matter against spirit, of barbarism against civilization. It is the "great heresy" of our age.

COMMUNISM, as might have been fore-seen, has in practice proved itself to be a theory of an anti-natural and profoundly anti-economic character.

COMMUNISM tends to subvert everything and, in its fury of destruction, it does not distinguish between error and truth, good and evil, justice and injustice. It cares not at all for history and the age-long experi-ence of humanity, for the life and dignity of human intelligence, for the pure affec-tions of family life, for the honour and modesty of woman, for the existence and greatness of nations, so long as it can, by its false conception of humanity, succeed in enslaving man and reducing him to the vilest abjection.

THE enemy has on his side money to buy consciences and arms, technical skill in overcoming difficulties, the eternal fascination of evil, absolute disregard of morals laws, and hatred, hatred of man, of fathers and sons, of woman, of intelligence, culture and goodness, a hatred which seems to be untiring and insatiable and spreads over unwary nations a black cloak of cruelty and terror.

CORPORATIVISM

THROUGH corporative organization, the economic life of the nation is an element of political organization.

IN organizing the economic corporations, one must keep in view that their interests, or rather the interests of production, must be subordinated to the interests of the national economy as a whole and also to the spiritual aims and high destiny of the nation and of the individuals who compose it.

IN contrast to what may be called the classical character of the financial reform, stands the economic and social revolution; and here too it seems that we need not turn back nor take another way, if we consider the benefits that have already accrued from the first ordering of our economy and the improvement attained in the conditions of labour.

THE professional syndicate is, through the homogeneity of interests within its sphere of production, the best basis for the organization of labour and the support, the fulcrum of the institutions which seek to raise and educate it and to protect it against injustice and adversity.

THERE can be no syndicate where there exists no corporative spirit, the consciousness of the value of labour in conjunction with production, an understanding of the necessity of cooperating with all the other factors with a view to the advancement of the economy of the nation. Where these qualities do not exist but only the spirit of class strife, there can be no true syndicate but only a revolutionary association using its strength in the service of disorder.

OUR
NATIONALISM

SPIRITUALITY

FROM a civilization which is scientifically returning to barbarism, we are irremissibly sundered by the spirituality which is the source, the soul, the life of our history.

CIVILIZATION

WE are the sons and heirs of an ancient civilization, whose mission it has been to educate and train the people to a higher idea of life, to form real men through the subjection of matter to spirit, of instinct to reason.

CONTINUITY

CRUSHED in the western strip of the Peninsula between powerful neighbours and the ocean, our existence is necessarily one long drama: but by the favour of Providence we can count eight centuries of toil and suffering, struggles and liberty, and if the danger remains the miracle remains also.

PORTUGAL

IT is a rare or unique thing in Europe and in all the world to be eight hundred years old, especially if the condition should be laid down that in the country in question, the people, the nation, the state should have remained the same. Almost from the beginning, by the achievements of the first

kings, our frontiers in the Iberian Peninsula were defined and fixed. Wars there
were many, but there was no invasion or
confusion of races or annexations of territory or changes of dynasty or alteration
of frontiers: from first to last, the leaders
of the nation had the same Portuguese
blood in their veins.

PORTUGAL was not made or united in
modern times nor took shape under the
pagan and anti-human ideal of deifying a
race or an empire. It was in the twelfth
and thirteenth centuries that she assumed
her present frontiers in the Iberian Peninsula, in the fifteenth and sixteenth centuries that she acquired vast dominions in
Africa, Asia, Oceania and America, defend-
ing Roman and Christian civilization
against Islam and spreading this civilization through new worlds. And this victory,
of transcendental importance to humanity,
was won by us at a time when the other
nations of Europe were immersed in the
strife of dynasties, schisms and heresies
which steeped them in blood.

EXEMPT from the disturbances in Europe,
where the modern states arose one after
another, Portugal saw many born, some
dismembered or incorporated with others

and not a few disappear. She survived them all, not "lost in the world's debate" but carrying out through the centuries of her existence one of the vastest enterprises, and one of the most beneficial to the common good of humanity, of which any people can boast. That is to say, she survived, not because she evaded life but because she lived the intense life of the soldier, the labourer on the land, the explorer on the sea, the discoverer, the missionary, the champion of a principle and of a civilization.

OUR WORK

SO far as our work concerns humanity, it spreads through the world; so far as it is national, it is essentially Portuguese.

OUR ASPIRATIONS

PORTUGAL is an old and free country, homogeneous in its structure, of frontiers unchanging almost since it became an independent state; a county which has shown itself peaceful in the troubled history of Europe but active on the sea, where its expansive force found vent in the discovery of new lands which it founded, colonized, civilized and incorporated in its own national existence. We are the sons of that past, and not in mere deference to the clearly expressed wishes of our ancestors

but in the knowledge that we are rendering a service to the peace of Europe and to
world civilization, we serenely assert our
will to be in the present and in the future
what we were in the past, free, independent, a nation of colonizers.

OUR ORIGINALITY

ONE day it will be recognized that Portugal
is governed by an original system, suitable to her history and geography, which
are very different from all others; and we
wish it might be understood that we have
not eschewed the mistakes and vices of a
false liberalism and a false democracy in
order to fall into others which might be
even worse, but rather to reorganize and
strengthen the country in the principles
of authority, of order, of the national traditions, reconciling these with those eternal
truths which are, happily, the heritage
of mankind and the crown of Christian
civilization.

THE PEOPLE

THE people are, in their simplicity of spirit
and spontaneity of sentiment, the ever
living source of our nationalism.

NATIONAL CONSCIENCE

HERE and afar we have right on our
side, the right of occupation, conquest,

discovery, and colonization, of the substance and blood of the Portuguese watering the earth in all parts of the world, cultivating the soil, opening up wastelands, trading, pacifying, instructing. It is the will of the people; it is the call of the national conscience.

THE NATION

NOTHING against the nation, everything for the nation.

LIKE a great family or a great concern, the nation, for the protection of its common interests and the attainment of its collective aims, requires a head to control it, a centre of life and action.

THE nation cannot be identified with a political party, a party is not the same as the state, and the state in international life is not a subject but a collaborator and associate.

THE man who becomes a nationalist belongs to no political party, no group or school: he makes use of materials according to their usefulness for the reconstruction of the country; his great, his only concern is that they should serve and become a part of the national system.

NONE of us, nationalists and lovers of our country, professes an aggressive nationalism of exclusiveness and hatred; rather, if we are attached to the idea of country, it is because our hearts and intellects instinctively tell us that the national sphere is still the best for the life and interests of humanity.

THIS is our theory and our position: an uncompromising but balanced nationalism, which simplifies the solution of the world's problems, taking advantage of its natural division into nations; and works with a clear understanding of international solidarity, to which it contributes with its actual achievements, and whose highest interests it does not injure or oppose by its activities in the national field.

THERE exist undoubtedly in the world political systems with which Portuguese nationalism has some resemblance and points of contact, most of which, indeed, are confined to the corporative idea but in actual practice, and especially in the conception of the state and in the organization of the political and civil support of the government, the differences are very marked.

WE have not failed to consider every foreign experiment, every series of facts occurring in any part of the world, with a view to extracting useful lessons from them. But the chief source of our instruction, the source of the inspiration of the main lines of our political structure, has been our history and traditions, the temperament and, in a word, the actual life of the Portuguese. From this source we seek to draw what of the past remains or should remain living and fruitful, and from the present that which seems a sure gain and the aspirations that are rendered legitimate by the general progress and by a better understanding of justice.

WITHOUT misgiving we make Portuguese nationalism the indestructible basis of the new state; first, because it is the clearest lesson of our history; secondly, because it is an inestimable factor in social progress and education; thirdly, because we are a living example of how the spirit of patriotism, displayed by us on every continent, has served the cause of humanity.

THE nationalism of the new state is not and can never be a doctrine of aggressive isolation, either of ideas or political theory, since, like all our history indeed, it has its roots in life and in friendly cooperation with other nations. We consider it as far removed from individualistic liberalism, which had a foreign origin, and from the internationalism of the Left, as from all other theoretic or practical systems which have sprung up abroad in reaction to them.

THE SUBSTANCE OF NATIONALISM

THE nation was formed almost at one blow, when this corner of the Peninsula was reconquered from the Moors, while our frontiers, which have remained unchanged for centuries, were not fixed at the expense of any other European nation. This fact withdraws us from the historical rivalries of conquests and enmities and allows the moral force of our independence and likewise of our expansion to stand out more clearly, since, after our position in the Peninsula had been consolidated, we crossed the seas in order to extend our dominions and show the world our genius as a civilizing power. Here is the innate and natural substance of this nationalism, which must be the soul of the preservation, regeneration and progress of Portugal.

IN THE RIGHT

IN this small western country which Europe had become accustomed to consider with pity or ennui, we have performed the miracle of reconstructing the nation in its traditional character, missionary and civilizing, chivalrous and spiritual; often we have had occasion, with our indisputable moral authority, to utter a word of reason in the councils of the great, and events have always proved that we were right.

THE SOLDIER

IT is the duty of us all to be true and just and patriotic; but, while the search for truth characterizes the learned, and the search for justice dominates the judge, it is patriotism that must absorb and dominate the spirit of the soldier.

THE ARMY

THE army has the secret of perpetual youth, and, as a great and ancient family of noble descent, it maintains and hands on its traditions so unimpaired and living that it always forms one and the same moral unity.

TWO things must be ever present to the mind of the armed forces: the first is that the basis of their organization and life is spiritual. All may not agree with the policy of the state or with certain administrative measures; but if honour and the nation disappear from the moral and intellectual disposition of the soldier, the army is left without rule or aim. The man who is against the nation cannot be a soldier. The second thing is this: in any compromise or neglect of this education or discipline the first victims will be the officers, for they must either fall in the exercise of their duty or suffer the inevitable penalties and undergo the consequences of their compliance and weakness.

THE
PORTUGUESE
EMPIRE

VOCATION

THE words "missionary vocation" have been applied to the universal and profoundly human tendency of the Portuguese people, inspired by its spirituality and disinterestedness.

UNIVERSALISM

UNIVERSALISM of idea and action in the course of Catholic and European evolution, directed towards the material and moral improvement of mankind: this is the main characteristic of the history of our country. It was in this spirit that we constructed noble bulwarks for the defence of the West in Morocco, colonized the Atlantic archipelagoes, built fortresses and factories along the coasts of Africa and the West, opened the way for the communications of all nations and created Brazil.

THE COLONIAL QUESTION

THE colonial question is a pressing problem of the day. The men who devote themselves to its study or are under the spell of the great anxieties caused by the colonial dominions are, by their ideas and proposals, sowing disquiet in the heart of several nations.

REFUSING any kind of bargain, we do not sell or give or lease or share our colonies, with or without reserving nominal sovereignty in a part of them to satisfy our national pride. The laws of our constitution forbid it, and, were there no such laws, it would be forbidden by the spirit of the nation.

IMPERIAL ECONOMY

I DO not forget that we also have the colonies as subsidiary elements in our economy, means of production, markets for our products and, within certain limits, an open field for the activity of our people; but in such circumstances and in the face of needs so serious both at home and in the colonies, I see only two elements for the solution of our problem: technical skill and organization, possibly technical skill through organization.

NEITHER in the mother-country nor in any of our colonies do we adopt an attitude of distrust or aggressiveness towards foreign capital, labour or initiative. More frankly than many other nations, we receive and welcome foreign collaboration. Throughout our empire many thousands of foreigners, many millions of foreign capital, work, prosper and shelter behind the generosity of our laws, the protection of our flag, the safeguard of our statutes and authority. But the elements which enter Portuguese territory in pursuit of their own advantage have to be considered by us as incorporated in the work of the nation, in Portuguese interests, as factors not of a foreign economy but of our own.

IMPERIAL UNITY

INDEED, we adopt the same criterion of a nation, a separate social unit, independent, sovereign, ordering as it chooses the division and organization of its territory, without distinctions of geographical position, in the way we consider, administer and govern the Portuguese colonies. As Minho or Beira, so is Angola or Mozambique or India, under the supreme authority of the state. We constitute a juridical and political unity, and we desire to attain an economic unity as complete and perfect as possible through developing the production and intensifying the exchange of raw materials, food products and manufactures between the various parts of this whole.

PORTUGAL and her overseas empire are a single unit, formed by the history of centuries on the face of the earth, to secure the independence, expansion, economic activity and communications of the first people which, at the cost of hard effort and sacrifice, sought out new worlds and oceans in order to enlarge its narrow dominion in Europe. The Portuguese of today must, by the force of their traditions, the strength of their enterprising people, the wise employment of their capital and credit, the coordination of their agricultural and industrial products, preserve and develop the whole of their possessions in the Iberian Peninsula, in Africa and in the East.

PORTUGAL
in
WORLD

DURING the next few years we, in common with others, will be entirely dominated by two great anxieties, the concern for peace and the concern of living; that is to say, problems of external politics and military defence, and problems of production and economic organization.

IN moments as ominous as the present for the peace of Europe and the destiny of nations, we must remain calm, but we may say that our chief anxiety is concerned with Portugal and western civilization.

THE WORLD'S SICKNESS

IT is above all the spirit of the world that is sick. From this western corner of the Peninsula we have long raised our weak voice to maintain this simple, sincere and, we trust, sensible contention.

THE CRISIS OF FEAR

THE truth which all feel and none dares to confess is that the world is living in a crisis of fear and that the general object of anxiety is to know how and in what sense the expansive force and genius of the great military powers will develop.

WHEN I survey the international panorama: the unrest, ruin and impoverish-
ment of the nations, their internal and
external strife, the disorder and indis-
cipline, the instability and weakness of
their governments, the irresoluteness of
principle, the social tension; when I think
that rich countries are unable to stabilize
their currency and that prosperous countries are unable or unwilling to meet their
debts, and great nations cannot balance
their budgets, when I see the crisis of life,
the crisis of wealth, the crisis of morality,
and then turn my eyes to our own house,
humble no doubt but quiet, orderly and
dignified, I feel that we should all be very
grateful to our national revolution.

EUROPE

EUROPE is disquieted and one of the signs
of its nervousness is the jealousy excited
by the ordinary manifestations of international friendships, and the need felt for
successive repetitions of these sentiments,
as though treaties and agreements were
not kept alive by trust in the pledged word
of State and had to be spoon fed with a
continual flood of sentimental words.

DURING recent years we have seen Europe grow very susceptible and rush after fantastic ideas which, after promising everything, yielded nothing. Locarno, Stresa, the United States of Europe, the Economic Conference of London, these are no longer hopes, they are ashes. And we cannot be sure that many are not even now running after illusions.

WAR

WAR is not a permanent state but rather the collapse of peace; hatred cannot be eternal, since the heart of man longs for love and is easily amenable to goodness; terror does not always paralyze will: a paroxysm of fear can beget contempt of life and deeds of heroism.

PEACE

PORTUGAL is a state which loves peace, possesses the spirit of civilization, collaborates in the strengthening of order in the world, stigmatizes wars of ambition, advocates arbitration to settle questions between states, fits its public law into the scheme of the higher aims of humanity, and seeks the harmonious, pacific, productive development of the faculties of its citizens with a view to the improvement and progress of the internal and external relations of the nation.

WE are pacific, but not pacifists; we are pacific collaborators with all nations for the good of humanity.

SOVEREIGNTY

Our sovereignty cannot be discussed at Geneva any more than it can be discussed in Paris, London, Rome or Berlin. Our sovereignty is our life, and of our life we alone can dispose.

THE LEAGUE OF NATIONS

THE League of Nations remodeled, renovated, with a different spirit and other methods of work, might even now be transformed into a useful juridical organ of international cooperation.

THE LUSITANIAN HOUSE

AS one who clears a piece of ground for cultivation and builds the walls of a house to dwell in, so many centuries ago great leaders marked out the boundaries with the sword and said "Here will we build the Lusitanian house."

HISTORY OF PORTUGAL

THE universality of ideas and actions in the course of Catholic and European evolution, directed towards the material and moral improvement of mankind: this is what characterizes the history of our country.

DIGNITY

WITHOUT excess or aggressiveness or quixotically declaring war upon the world, countries, like individuals, can, by their hard work and their virtues, have the right to stand, the poor before the rich and the little before the great, with head high and even with their hat upon their head.

PRESTIGE

ONE may say without exaggeration that our international situation is better than it has been for several decades: the atmosphere of expectation and later of curiosity concerning Portuguese revolutions has been exchanged for an atmosphere of affection, nay, of prestige.

TWO incontestable facts, which can easily be verified and are not liable to the confusions of party faction, warrant the legitimate pride of the Portuguese on either side of the Atlantic: the new internal prestige and the new external prestige of Portugal.

FOREIGN POLICY

THE traditional course of our foreign policy, that in keeping with the true interests of Portugal is: to avoid as far possible, being embroiled in European conflicts, in maintaining friendship with Spain, in developing the possibilities of our power in the Atlantic.

WHILE Portugal itself is a narrow strip of Europe which can never contain more than a few million souls, Brazil is almost a continent, a new world, from which through the centuries to come will pour torrents of men, to whose hands may confidently be entrusted the treasure of the traditions which they will inherit, sharing with us this sacred trust.

BRITISH ALLIANCE

ALLIANCES involve rights and obligations on either side. Our alliance with Great Britain will gain in strength the more those rights and obligations balance on each side of the scales.

TO those who ask me if I believe in England and in the British alliance, I answer frankly and sincerely that I do: in the first place, because I believe in the plighted word of men and nations so long as there are no facts to challenge my belief; and, secondly, because, even apart from our close ties of friendship, the community of Portuguese and British interests is so evident that for a long time to come statesmen in both countries must be governed by this fact.

ALPHABETICAL INDEX

A

Action 8
Administration 27
Anxieties 71
Army 61
Aspirations 55
Authority 21
Authority and liberty 21

B

Brazil 76
British alliance 76

C

Certainties 3
Choice 8
Civilization 53
Colonial question 65
Colonies 66
Communism 47
Confidence 3
Conscience (national) 56
Continuity 53
Corporative Chambers 16
Corporativism 48
Crisis 40
Criticism 17

D

Democracy 14
Destitution 43
Devotion 6
Difficulties 3
Dignity 75
Doctrine 23

E

Economy (Imperial) 66
Economy in the service of man 41
Economy (Political) 39
Economy (State and) 39
Education 35
Education (Physical) 36
Enemy 47
Europe 72
Example 28

F

Faith 3
Fallacies 15
Family (the) 34
Family (House and) 35
Fear (The crisis of) 71
Finances (Reform of the) 28
Frankness 5

G

Gaiety 7
Government 24
Government (State and) 12

H

History of Portugal 74
House and family 35
House (The Lusitanian) 74

I

Ideas 7
Illusion 39
Imperial unity 67
Improvements 42
Irresponsibility 6

J

Justice 5
Justice (Social) 42

L

Laws 24
Leadership 26
League of Nations 74
Liberalism 13
Liberty 21
Liberty (Authority and) 21
Life 33

M

Methods 28
Men 34
Money 40
Morality 6
Morality (State and) 12

N

Nation 57
Nation (The Sovereignty of the) 12
Nationalism 58
Nationalism (The substance of) 60
Needs (Essential) 33
Newspapers 17

O

Opinion (Public) 17
Order 21
Originality 56

P

Panorama 72
Parliaments 16
Peace 73
People 56
Plutocrats 42
Policy 26
Policy (Administrative) 27
Policy (Foreign) 75
Politicians 25
Politics 26
Portugal 53
Portugal (History of) 74
Prestige 75
Production (State and) 40
Property 43

R

Reason 5
Regimes 13

Responsibility 5
Revolution 23
Revolutions 23
Right 60

S

Sacrifice (Self) 7
Salaries 46
School 36
Sense (Good) 4
Seriousness 7
Sickness (The world's) 71
Sincerity 4
Slavery (Modern) 42
Socialism 14
Soldier 61
Sovereignty 74
Spirituality 53
Stability 15
State 11
State and economy 39
State and Government 12
State and morality 12
State and production 40
State (Power of the) 40
State and wealth 40
Strength 22
Strife (Class) 46
Syndicates 49
System (The representative) 16

T

Task 28

Tenacity 8
Truth 4

U

Universalism 65

V

Values 6
Values (National) 33
Vocation 65

W

War 73
Wealth (State and) 40
Will 8
Work 43
Working classes 45
Workmen's families 45

Y

Youth 36

www.ingramcontent.com/pod-product-compliance
Lightning Source LLC
Chambersburg PA
CBHW021003150626
46549CB00012BA/1012